MUSSOLINI

MUSSOLINI

THE LAST 600 DAYS OF IL DUCE

RAY MOSELEY

TAYLOR TRADE PUBLISHING
Dallas • Lanham • Boulder • New York • Toronto • Oxford

Published by Taylor Trade Publishing
An imprint of The Rowman & Littlefield Publishing Group, Inc.
4501 Forbes Boulevard, Suite 200
Lanham, MD 20706

Distributed by NATIONAL BOOK NETWORK

Library of Congress Cataloging-in-Publication Data
Moseley, Ray, 1932–
  Mussolini : the last 600 days of il Duce / Ray Moseley.
    p. cm.
Includes bibliographical references and index.
  ISBN 1-58979-095-2 (cloth : alk. paper)
  1. Mussolini, Benito, 1883–1945. 2. Heads of state—Italy—Biography.
3. Fascism—Italy—History. 4. Italy—Politics and
government—1914–1945. I. Title.
DG575.M8M66 2004
945.091'092—dc22

                                        2003026579

Manufactured in the United States of America.

CONTENTS